for Vera

1

Prism of My Mind

Poems for seven moods

By

Francis C. Mont

Published by Montland Books in 2015

ISBN-13: 978-0-9949094-2-8
ISBN-10: 099490942X

Cover Photo by:
© Mopic | Dreamstime.com

The Author

Francis Mont has been living in Canada for the last 50 years, after he emigrated from his native Hungary where he studied science and received a degree in Theoretical Physics. However, it was easier to make a living in Computer Science where he did research, application and teaching over the years.

He is interested in profound questions, both in science and in social philosophy. He is a 'big picture' person, focusing on fundamental principles and the defining essence of the topic at hand. In particular he is passionate about the issues of social organization and justice, and the individual's relationship to the planet and to the human species.

He also pursues independence and self reliance to the best of his abilities, as his solar power system and year-around greenhouse demonstrate.

He writes poetry, plays classical violin, dabbles at wood carving and has not yet stopped building the house he and his wife and (currently) five cats live in.

Contents

Hope

The blue heron

The blue heron conjured itself
out of hot shimmering air,
or maybe it just floated up from the marsh
by the greyish-blue band of the road I was driving on.
It did not seem to fly, just hovered
with lazy indifference to the gravity
binding me to the ground.

It was huge: all wings, neck and legs,
yet it had the beauty of the improbable:
all curves carrying a head,
mostly just beak:
a feathery mosquito
with a five-foot wingspan.

Herons are so mysterious,
so rare,
an omen, a sign,
a revelation with great importance -
I asked what message it brought
to a human on a quest.

It did not reply directly,
just kept ahead of me,
out of reach,
transcending the obvious and predictable
to something almost completely unknown,
yet frighteningly familiar.

It seemed to say:
existence is not uniquely human,
the 'god' we blame
made us all part of the puzzle,
with equally significant roles
in teaching one another
about beauty, truth
and harmony in the universe.

I thanked him for this piece
I have been missing
through a lifetime of trying to understand -
the obvious answer to an age-old question:
It's not all about us, people,
it is about life…
…we are just a small
and not always important part.

It's about being, loving, dying,
reborning and retrying,
forever,
or until we finally,
one day,
realize
that we are not that different
from anything alive
on this planet,

we are not many, but
we are
only
one.

Dreamers

Faraday was the first
who saw the invisible lines:
a force field permeating all of magnetic space.
He didn't know he was proven right
by the Aurora Borealis;
he only knew that iron filings
sprinkled on a sheet of paper,
made, for him, the lines visible.
Many thought that it was risible
to imagine such things:
if you couldn't see them, couldn't touch them,
how could they exist?

Einstein imagined space
filled with clocks ticking away,
at their own speed, in their own way.
Time flows at a different rate
for you and me if we don't wait
for each other but speed away
in opposite directions.
No one understood
his wild contention.

Sagan imagined the stars
we might visit some day
from our "pale blue dot"
and find new planets orbiting
in elliptical paths,
some teeming with life, intelligence.

Then we'd know we are not alone,
that the whole universe
is our home.

All these dreamers shared this:
they were not afraid to dream,
to look beyond what may seem
rock-solid reality.

They knew there had to be
glorious variety in the cosmos:
in boundless infinity.

They are all dead now
but I still talk to them,
ask if I could share their vision...
...and they say that dreams are still free
and that's the way
it should,
forever,
be.

First birthday

Today my grown-up mind is banished
to the painful awareness of tomorrows,
because today has to be innocent, clean,
suitable for the glorious birthday
of a one-year-old,
who believes us to be gentle, loving beings,
surrounding her like an embrace
of benevolent, warm affection.

Today I will celebrate the 'could-have-been',
the still unspoilt marble or canvas of creation
that started so well,
promising us David and the Sistine Chapel,
before the chisel slipped
or the brush mugged up in the creator's hand,
producing this tragic, disfigured,
crippled creature we are,
with breathtaking beauty
and horrifying ugliness
merged into one.

Today I want to forget the accident,
close my eyes and see the monster transformed
into beauty, peace, compassion, honour
and, of course,
intelligence that we need to cope with our demons:
our ugly little impulses, jealousies, fears
that we inherited
from our terrifying history of survival,
against all odds,
against a relentless, indifferent nature.

Today I want to be like the boy was,
now lying broken at the bottom of a memory well,
buried so deep under years of
already knowing better:
I want to relive the excitement, wonder
of discovering benevolent nature,
and the power of the human mind
comprehending, coping, transforming
all unknowns to familiar and safe.

And, just like you wash up,
don your best suit, comb your hair
and cleanse your soul before entering church
for your Sunday worship
of a merciful, all-loving 'god':
with my mind emptied of all knowledge
of pain, brutality and ugliness,
I will be ready to face
the clean mind of an innocent child,
celebrating one year
of unsullied existence.

Fog

The morning fog painted my sky
with grey, wet, April branches
shivering in the wind like skeletons of past summers,
like bent old men remembering their youth -
I feel my age today.

My mind drifts into familiar grooves of despair,
knowing too much so easily turns into gloom...
...the fog will do it any old time:
a perfect envelope for pessimistic thoughts.
I wish that sunshine of yesterday
lasted a bit longer - I so enjoyed the illusion of spring.

The news were bad last night,
like the wet fog,
they surround everything...
...it's hard to see evolution
when we repeat mistakes from
decades, centuries and millennia ago.

With a conscious effort of will
I close my eyes and remember a different day
when the sun set my heart on fire,
embracing the trees in golden halo,
offering beauty, promising peace.

In life, I have learned by now,
everything comes in pairs:
light and darkness,
warm - cold,
love - hate;
good and evil;
birth and demise...

...I have free will
to bask
in either side:
it's up to me,
it has always been so.

Hate and Compassion

We may think our hate avenges some victim,
rights some wrong,
balances an evil,
we may believe our cause is just
and we have to hurt those back
who have hurt us.

But, sooner or later,
we grow tired of anger and hate
(it takes so much out of us)
and search for redeeming factors,
excuses and circumstances
to spare us the tear and wear
of destructive emotions.

Admit it, old chap,
you have slowed down, mellowed,
do everything now with new-found moderation:
your love is a warm, autumn glow,
your appetite is not ravenous,
and your capacity for hate
is seriously diminished.

Now you make excuses
for villains you hated before;
you tell yourself:
we are all victims here,
one way or another,
There is no original sin -
we were all dear babies once.

Luck influences who you've become:
smart or stupid,
healthy or sick,
good or evil -

something must have made you one
or the other -
we must never stop thinking
of causes and effects.

If you can maintain this vision,
this tolerance, this understanding,
then your anger yields to pity, sorrow
for all victims of the human condition -
your heart will find peace
in serenity, acceptance, compassion.

But, alas,
so many of us cannot forgive,
piling pain upon pain,
death upon death...
...victims victimizing,
infinitely, relentlessly,
and thus hate is perpetuated,
until love has finally lost,
until hate has consumed all its fuel:
the last of us.

Hovering
(inspired by Barbara Kingsolver's "Animal Dreams")

I have been hovering
over life,
looking for a perch
strong enough for my weight,
light enough to sway in the breeze,
high enough to give me a view,
safe from the teeth,
safe from the claws.

A perfect place,
protected from sharp winds;
some shade but not too much,
so the sun could warm my heart
before the long, cold night
of oblivion.

I'm still looking
though my wings are tired,
though each new place
seems a poorer one,
even though I'm losing hope,
running out of time,
out of choice.

I wish I could go back
to my youth of un-squandered resources
and start again,
with a lot more tolerance,
a lot less pride,
a little more wisdom.

Any day now
I'll have to take a chance on landing,
touch and be touched...
...long enough to sing my song
about beauty, awe and wonder,
about the gift of having seen,

having felt,
having been,
for this fleeting moment
between the not yet
and the not anymore...

Ready or not,
here I am,
here is home.

Nightmare

Walking along
the broken pavement
of my ever-recurring dream,
I want to run,
as I choke on a scream.

The terror starts
as terrors always do:
in the darkness,
a point of light,
growing larger, closer, brighter,
filling up the night.

I know it will kill me
with a thunderous crash,
roll over my body
with a mind freezing dash
into the horizon behind me
leaving the road
dark and empty...

Without clues for
where it came from,
to where it leaves,
I wonder for the thousandth time
as I wake up, gasping for air,
what this means.

Have not had this dream for decades,
lost in the fog of the past --
I must have heeded
unknown warning,
avoiding a self-destructive path

Entropy

Birds on the feeder,
deer found our offering...
...entropy delayed.

Sleepwalker

I could have become
like most people:
take the world for granted,
accept it and
drift with the flow
or hate it and fight it –
but I chose to become a sleepwalker,
treat the real as a bad dream
and when awake – dream on.

All my dreams are naive,
woven on the loom of childhood stories,
sweet fairy tales,
where good is rewarded,
talent given scope,
diligence promoted.
People are friends,
helping;
loyalty, honour and fairness
are important values
that everyone lives by
(except for the bad guys,
always defeated).

When finally my childhood ended
and I was ready to live
my adult life – unprotected
for the first time,
I took a good look
and decided:
my dreams had no chance
in the real world.

I had to choose,
so I escaped
back to my dreams.

I don't know if it was wisdom,
cowardice or just simple
pig-headed stubbornness
guiding me. I only know that
it means more to me
to maintain this dream,
to be true to myself
than all the rewards,
recognitions, riches
and promotions
this 'real' world
could offer me.

I'm not a hero,
I don't do this to please 'god',
don't hope for reward
in some afterlife, but
it is the most profoundly selfish act
of seeking pleasure
in the immediate moment –
I can claim my life is
what dreams
are made of.

Last Man

The last man on Earth was devastated,
sitting alone in his room.
He had spent a lifetime
arguing with whom
he could corner
and now none could hear him any longer
because he was the last of his kind
and no one would remember
all the truths he ever stated.

They, the others, all died,
not knowing cause and effect,
confusing the rock-solid fact
with wishful delusion,
ignoring the basic laws
of human evolution.

He knew only of another
non-delusional mind:
he called her his soulmate,
not daring to hope
she could still be alive --
he whispered: never more...

when he heard this heart-wrenchingly
lovely sound:

a hesitant knock on the door.

Communication

Communication is an art,
a science, a hopeless human quest:
an attempt to reach our brother,
trying to breech the abyss that keeps us apart,
finding ourselves in the mind of another.

Cigarette break

The exhaustion washes over me in nauseating waves
as I lean back in my chair, close my eyes...
...the yellow pool of the desk lamp's light
casts a shadow on the wall behind...
...my shade following my every move.

I light up, adding the tiny, dancing flame of the lighter
to the mood of mild apprehension,
brought into focus by the red glow of the cigarette.
A distant, racial memory of some ancient ritual:
flickering amber in the dark,
haunts the room inside.

Thoughts are nudged, herded in my mind,
trying to penetrate the veil of the past, of the future,
but all I am aware of is the present.
Maybe this moment is all I have,
without a before or an after...
...and yet, it is the future I would like to see
where my path will take me from here.

The future is approaching, closer,
with every heartbeat, with every blink of an eye,
and, as the smoke slowly wafts across the air,
so is my destiny, coming, ready to envelop me
in the yet unknown, hoped-for, feared,
promising nothing,
flowing, inexorably, from future to past.

Work is awaiting, more tomorrows,
more hopes, struggles, victories, defeats...
Minutes arrive, then vanish behind me,
and whatever my fate is
will be a day closer tomorrow.

Tribe within a tribe

Tribe within a tribe within a tribe,
a maddening nesting of Matryoshka,
who can keep track of the obligation
one has to each generation.

I must be a good husband, a good citizen,
a good employee, a perfect gentleman,
and when my tribe tells me to fight
I have to go and bleed in the night.

Why can't we just have only one tribe
that all of us belong to – dammit
the tiger has only one kind of stripe
there is no reason to complicate it.

We are all human, on this forsaken planet
stuck in the same boat on the ocean,
if we keep fighting tribe against tribe
we will never have a moment
of peace, when we can love each other...

...forget the stupid tribes and learn to live together!

The illusion of life

I have heard it said
that life is a river...
...when we wake up at birth
time starts flowing
as a small stream,
gushing down the mountain,
gathering strength, growing, growing,
meandering across the plains,
meeting tributaries,
slowing down as it approaches the ocean
and quietly merging into the sea.
...
Life is one very long day,
with minutes ticking away...
...we have the illusion
of a new beginning
when we spring out of bed
ready, yet again,
to conquer the world...
...each nap helping us forget
how futile, how pointless
this day-long existence is.
...
Life is a book - an adventure tale...
...we keep turning pages,
one day at a time,
prepared for surprises,
boredom, resolution,
fear, happiness, love,
following the writer's whim
helplessly, unable
to put it down.

One of these days
I will understand life
before it is over,
before I must close the book,
end the day,
say hello to the ocean,
merge into oblivion
and leave behind
this heartbreakingly beautiful
illusion.

Humour

Ageing

Age creeps up on me,
stealing me blind,
now I need glasses;
driving on the road
I am so slow,
every old lady passes.

My joints are shot
my hearing's so bad
you have to say
everything twice.
My hair's getting thin,
but thrives in the nose:
this is not very nice.

My elbow hardly bends,
my fingers always ache,
don't even mention my neck!
I don't run any more,
shuffle is more likely...
...admit it: I am an old wreck.

It isn't so bad,
when I consider:
I'm not really losing -

because, as I age,
with less and less 'can-do'
less and less seems worthwhile doing.

Evolution

While thumbing his phone
he walks into a lamp post.
Evolution sighs.

I am sixty

When I was six,
my mother convinced me
I was a genius, a poet, a musician
rolled into one.

It was fun
to believe those things –
no-one suggested
what I needed
was talent,
a little inspiration
and a lot of – sweating
(perspiration is a better word,
but has been already done).

Still, I dabbled at things
over the decades that followed:
I tried the violin from six to sixteen,
and even though you could recognize
the pieces I played,
Oistrakh, Menuhin and Perlman
just played on.

At sixteen I fell in love -- on schedule --
and, naturally, became a poet;
hunting for rhymes and cadence
to impress the girl
with my eloquence...
...She did have the patience
to hear me out,
but had to interrupt,
to leave for her wedding.

At last, it dawned on me
that science was my calling
because I knew Einstein was wrong,
so "it's Physics where I belong",
I told myself hotly
and I spent the next six years
getting me a degree...
...Einstein just slumbered on.

Finally, I turned to computers:
this is my cup of tea (I thought)
and for the next thirty-two years
even if I didn't put Bill Gates out of a job:
it was a living.
(my mother's assurance fast receding
into a thick, merciful fog).

At thirty-six
my wife bought me chisels,
so I tried a dolphin, a penguin, an eagle,
and in each case,
(as with the violin)
you could actually recognize
what they were meant to resemble.

Today, I am sixty.
and, after fifty-four years of trying,
I can admit with assurance:
my mother was wrong.

I am not a genius, a poet,
a musician all rolled into one –
but I am not complaining:
I've had fifty-four years
of never-ending fun.

The last man on Earth

The last man on Earth
sat alone in his room,
aware of his isolation,
knowing He would come for him soon
with his well-deserved salvation.

There was a knock on the door
and he eagerly rushed to answer,
wondering why He was late...
...but he saw only hooves, tail and horn,
sealing his misanthropic fate.

Reverse-land

Now I live in reverse-land
where everything is upside down:
reverse seventy-one -- you get seventeen,
reverse serious and you get
an old hippy, a silly clown.

In normal-land I'm past
the best years I remember,
my eyes are dim,
my hair is grey,
my knees always tender.

In reverse land I thrive,
seeking new adventure:
write a book on science;
play with violin,
poetry,
sculpture.

As I age in normal-land,
in reverse-land I grow ever younger,
soon I will be a child again:
innocent, happy, curious,
in my world of magic and wonder.

I don't really mind
reversing ravages
time has done to my pride...
...soon I will surrender
to the illusion
...lean back in my rocking chair,
enjoying the ride.

A soap on a rope

Earth is like a soap on a rope
twirled around by the sun,
year after year,
in an endless run.

I wonder if the sun is aware
how sick, how beyond hope
how badly infested by us
this poor globe is at the end of the rope.

If I were the sun
I wouldn't want to know…
…I would open my hand;
let the poor bastards go.

You ain't dead yet

You ain't dead yet,
the clown said to the waif
hoping to cheer him up...
...but the bum didn't wait
for the explanation,
but hit him for a buck
for a dram of whisky,
to forget he was alive,
hoping the memory would fade
by the time the effect wore off.

Joy

Beauty

The whitewash of fresh, pillowy snow
meets the milky fog of the sky,
as ghostly shapes of winter birds
float in the air, weightless like a dream,
before they alight on the feeder.

I let this improbable beauty
soak into my soul,
wipe my mind clean
of pessimistic thoughts --
it surrounds me like sweet memory
of a lover's embrace
from a happier past.

I will try to hold on to this feeling
in the coming days of poisonous news
of a world gone mad --
try to remember that beauty does still exist
and not everything is hopelessly sad.

First snow

Snowflakes dance in air,
turning all that's dark to light...
...whitewashing our sins.

Flowerpot Island

The forest was wild
with moss-covered rocks and trees,
in a battle neither could win...
...they were frozen in a fused mass
of life and matter:
cedar and dolomite
coexisting
since forever.

Trees growing in fissures,
giant boulders blocking their path,
slanting rays of a ghostly sun
penetrating the dark.

Deep caves yawning above
in the looming rock face,
with wild pigeons flitting about
and blind bats in the ink-coloured space.

The trail snaked higher and higher,
cut into the unyielding soil,
woven through with twisted, hard roots
reaching to trip a careless foot.

The air was still, not a sound
disturbed this ancient space,
images of long gone cavemen
invaded my wandering mind:
ancestors of an indestructible race.

I was mesmerized with awe and wonder
over nature naked and true,
and from the lap of a civilized world
I was briefly reunited with the past,
the unforgiving millennia,
that my species had to come through.

What's what

I have heard it said that suffering is good for us.
Never believed it for a second!
Whoever thought of such a crazy thing
needs to hear it from me, on the record,

the simple truth that nothing can change:
pleasure is good and pain is not...
...just ask a gerbil, a cat or a dog
they will tell you what's what.

I could live for a thousand years,
expanding my mind with science,
reveling in nature and the arts
and being creative, as far as

my talents allow me to go,
dabbling in all kinds of things,
having nothing but pleasure in life
until the final bell rings.

Life

I am touching the wall
next to my bed
and revel in having a hand...
...texture, warmth, flatness to feel,
caress and greedily possess...

I walk on the grass,
my naked feet touch green, succulent blades:
I can stand, jump, crouch,
what a joy it is
to move over the planet!

I breathe and take air in, deep,
surrounded... in it... around it,
love to have lungs...
...love to have, still, life to live.

I am the old man,
and the baby,
and the space-suited ghost
in 2001...now 2011,

I am the child I used to be,
the young lover,
the poet,
the man on my death bed,
soon enough,
fading away...

I am my father
I quarreled with over nothing,
I am my mother,

who loved me more than
it should be possible to love,
I am my brother who found 'god'
and I am my sister
who found nothing.

I am all of you, out there,
reading these lines,
wondering what it is
I am trying to say:
Please, love life and love each other
as the only thing that matters,
as the only thing you can leave behind,
as the only thing you can take with you
at the end.

Planting

Black, moist earth covers old fingers -
gnarled, curly reeds,
as I prepare the bed for kernels to plant,
I contemplate the life hiding in the seeds
a force that only gods can grant.
I am not a gardener, a green-fingered creature,
only an amateur following a scripture.

All life starts in such a mysterious way
with a seed being germinated.
I can't help but think of how I may
have been born, created
by my parents who desired, in their mind,
to plant their consciousness within a child.

Maybe all life on Earth was a gift of an alien culture,
setting a beautiful force into motion,
giving the sun, the dirt, the water structure,
launching an evolution.

Hummingbirds

Hummingbirds dancing,
grace colours my window frame:
summer's gift to me.

Saturn

The pale, pastel-pink globe,
embraced by jaunty rings,
on a vast, star-studded sky,
drifted, slowly
across my viewfinder.

Earth slowly rotated
under my feet,
summer-dawn breeze
gently ruffled my hair...

Saturn was there, immutable,
following its path of causes and effects,
and I thought of Galileo,
who laboured over a block of glass,
grinding it into a lens,
to behold the same planet...

...and, through a gap of four hundred years,
he and I
looked into each other's eyes.

Love

Christmas

Celebrations are
time out from daily grind...
...love wins for a day.

Black cat

The black cat
sits on the arm of my chair,
very comfortably indeed.
A thin piece of his hair
stuck to the pen I am holding,
as a reminder,
a strand
tying us together.

He is warm, friendly,
a living thing,
like I am,
with fears, affections
and a need to share
and communicate.

His back is turned towards me,
suggesting indifference...
...but I know better:
he depends on me
as I do - on him.

Warm, soft, vulnerable,
maybe we have a lot more in common
than this interdependence...
...maybe it is life,
shared and divided,
holding us together.

A soft, purring sound
is the only sign of his being alive,
and I drink it in
as if it were survival.

I love this cat
because he's so human,
so much like me
that it scares me a little.

Is this all we are?
Are we reduced
to our hopes, needs, fears?
Is everything else
only pretence? ...

...Maybe it just doesn't matter,
maybe it is enough
to be soft and cuddly.

Hope

I wasn't prepared
to see you smile,
to see you frown,
to see you cry.
I wasn't prepared
to meet you yet,
to believe, to hope,
to want to try.

Your voice is soft, solemn,
promising so much to say.
A ray of light,
warm patch of gold,
erupting into the cold,
into the grey.

It shakes me hard,
I panic to think:
you may be true,
could be the one.
Run, I would
if I had the strength,
courage to dare
become my own
executioner.

I know,
I know you hardly yet.
I may be wrong,
long is the path
we have to climb.
The ray of light
I think I feel

could be reflection
from my heart.

I feel the pain
you try to hide,
wish I could hold your hand,
caress your hair,
wish you were brave to cry.
Why the pride,
why not share
with one
who wants to care?

Exciting games,
sparkling wit,
brilliant brain
I do not seek to find.
I want to hold a human hand
who needs my need,
touches my soul,
answers my mind.

Fear

If you wonder,
once in a while,
whether the words:
'we are true friends'
mean the same to both you and me,
I have to say: I do not know.

Words that echo
inside my head
are 'honesty', 'trust', 'loyalty'
and 'concern' and yes, 'interest';
commitment to another soul,
one I deeply care about...
...but I must be dishonest,
or at least confused:
because I left something out
from the picture
and it must be there too, somewhere,
if truth be told.

The word I tried so hard to miss
is a word so terrifying,
that I needed all my power
to call it forth:
such a short and innocent word:
I'll say it now:
'Fear'...
...you see,
I have said it.
it is not a gaping abyss
under my feet,
not a threat of crumbling to dust,
it's a word of letters, it seems,
picked randomly,

lightly dismissed
and forgotten.

No, I'm lying.
The word is still there:
'Fear'...
...of dying,
of loneliness,
futility,
infinity of space and time,
and the fear of losing my mind.

Nightmare vision:
drifting through space
spinning slowly,
falling, falling,
no beginning,
no end in sight
of a journey
to the end
of limitless time.

I think: 'friendship' was invented
by a castaway like that spaceman:
to hold fast to his sanity,
last remaining shred of his mind.
He imagined the distant stars,
tiny points of blinking light
were his soul mates,
sharing his fate,
watching his path,
loving him as
the desperate
and the condemned
can only love
before they died.

And yet, and still,
friendship must mean more than fear,
because I know :
I could face, and I could defy
all the horrors,
I could throw my body and mind
into harm's way,
into pain and into fire...
...if only with this final act
I could save you,
my beloved,
my dearest friend...
...if only the moment of death
could give me what
I never had:
purpose,
meaning,
destination,
deliverance,
my completion,
my peace of mind.

I want to be the one

I want to be the one to tell you:
it's beautiful to be alive.
Climb up the hills; swim, cross the lake;
rake the leaves into big piles
over your kids, laughing with joy;
watch the ants toil under heavy loads and make it;
follow your whim where it flies.

I want to be the one to tell you:
your world is safe; your truth is true;
the sun shines through the leaves of the tree
you feel holds you doomed forever
to follow your lonely path;
you are free to build your shelter for injured birds
whose broken wings need to mend:
you will find me there to give you a hand.

I want to be the one to tell you:
that magic is true,
that you need not listen to lies,
that some mirrors always laugh.
I want you to believe:
it is worth to travel the length...
...and if you do:
it will give me the strength..

Guilt

(Dedicated to Margaret Atwood and Vera who
introduced me to her work)

'God' made me a man,
(in his image – at least that's what they say)
and there's nothing that I can do.
Besides, why would I want to change it
when I enjoy all the advantages
that come with the title?
...women were just a frivolous afterthought,
an addendum to amuse me,
serve, spoil, and stroke my ego,
mirror to reflect my heroic stance,
long eye-lashes fluttering
like wings of whimsical butterflies
and then lowered demurely.
This is what 'god' intended -
can't you see?

Just say something!
don't look at me accusingly,
don't be such a goddamn martyr!
for Christ's sake, don't fear me!
Have I ever threatened you or hurt you
even in the tiniest way?
Yes, I know: I could hurt you.
I am stronger.
I have muscles bunched up on my arms and shoulders
arms that could grab, tear, choke, strangle.
weight that could crush, smother and suffocate,
penis that could stab, plunge and violate...
...but it isn't my fault
that you are so small and fragile, so delicate,
and so breathtakingly beautiful and vulnerable.
You can't hold it against me that you are so weak
and you have been raped so often,
it's not my fault.

Please,
don't torment me
with this guilt that tears me apart!
Can we make peace?
pretend we are equal, pretend that 'god'
did not base his design on the food chain
where the strong can and will devour the weaker
as a matter of course,
as a matter of survival.

And if we can maintain this myth,
for an afternoon stroll in the garden,
arm in arm,
and head against a non-threatening shoulder,
then, perhaps,
for one magic and enchanted moment,
we can both feel healed, completed,
we can both forgive
and forget...

...till the next time
when I say something stupid
that will hurt you -
even though,
I could and would die without hesitation
to protect you from any harm...
...because you are what's best in me
you are what gives meaning to my pointless existence,
makes my life not entirely futile,
because,
as long as I possess and hold
something as beautiful and precious
as the love of someone like you
I can feel peace,
I can feel
redeemed,
forgiven
and
guiltless.

Happiness

'God',
I don't know what it all means,
and I do have plenty to be mad about:
blame you for the hate, suffering,...
...but today,
I am disarmed by the enormous gift
you bestowed on me last night
when, for an unexpected moment,
you made me glad
to be alive.

It wasn't much,
just a simple statement:
'but of course, I love you, Francis';
just a look of pleasure, peace, contentment...
...she does mean everything to me
in this confused, sad world.

This love,
this certainty,
non-negotiable faith
and non-relative truth
saves me from drowning
in the tide of anger and pain,
of evil and stupidity...
...
for a precious Sunday morning
out of place, out of time,
I can nurture this soft, gentle glow,
this absolute, this happiness,
and for that,
I do thank you,
'God'.

I love my cat

He is so small, even for a cat,
innocent, full of purr and love,
brave, honest, playful,
and so grateful
for the home he got.

There is not a one
deceitful bone in his hide,
he tells me exactly what's on his mind,
he knows when I am sad,
and also when I am mad at him
for his little sins he can't resist,
even though I told him so many times
please, leave my pencil alone,
this is *my* chair, desist!

I can pick him up by his scruff,
hang him upside down,
he knows it's just human stuff
and the infinite trust
he honours me with
makes us the closest you can be with a friend
a real love you can never pretend.

Identity

In this age of uncertainty,
it's so hard to know who we really are.
Roles we have tried
lie discarded in our wake
like snake skins we outgrew...
Most of us are bare or mottled,
waiting for the new skin to hold,
hide and protect us a while.

When you came, I was recently
stripped more naked
than I had ever been before.
I quickly grabbed
the nearest role,
hiding behind flimsy façades,
I hoped you would not see through me
and run away.

You stayed...
...gently healing wounded ego,
confused mind and jumbled feelings,
till I was free to look at me,
take stock, unearth
layer after layer of the "I" that you knew
hid there under heaps of rubble,
for both of us to discover.

Like anyone,
I was born with an open script:
talents, promises, handicaps,
danger signs and missing pieces.
It took some time, but now I know

who I have been,
who I am and, quite certain,
who I can be
in the precious
remaining time.

When I will finish my life,
I will not die rich and famous,
not one of my abilities
developed to full potential -
but when it comes,
I'll die content,
knowing that I avoided
what I feared most
in my darkest
premonitions.

I will die as most of us do:
unfinished art, unsung hero,
brave starts
and some accomplishments.
But, thanks to you,
I will not die like a sad fool
who never knew
who he was and what he saw
in this land of mystery and tragedy
of glorious and triumphant Life.

Mother

Even in death,
her hair smelled freshly washed sweet
when I kissed it, for the last time.
The crumpled-up-little-face
of that bottomless night
relaxed into peaceful, innocent sleep,
and I almost made a mental note
to have coffee ready when she woke up.

Yes, I know, she won't wake up anymore
to a day of unpretentious joy;
animals, plants,
clean, tidy, pretty things in her world
and in other people's minds,
in other people's hearts.

She owned the sunset
painting her window wild and subtle,
showed it off with pride,
sharing with us so many times.
She was delicate,
I teased her with the "pea and the princess"
and she accepted my tribute,
sipping cold coffee from slim china cup.

She was a peacemaker,
smoother of ruffled feathers,
generous, forgiving, quick to love,
troubled by anger, resentment,
anyone's pain of any kind.
In others she accepted weakness,
forgave mistakes,

encouraged with soft words,
sunburst-radiant smile.

She was my Mother in every true sense but one,
and the two of them would have liked each other:
two imps, butterfly spirits,
dancing, singing, laughing
through hardships and happier times,
making good-natured fun of everything,
never able to resist a punch-line.

Before she died I asked how one could bottle all this,
how one could preserve love, humour, sweetness
beyond the grave,
and I sadly realized:
these are things you can take with you,
leaving vast, empty holes behind
in aching hearts,
in longing minds.

I wish I could hug her one more time,
peck a small kiss on her white hair under my chin,
tell her how much magic, humour,
all embracing goodness she had brought into my life
when she asked, shyly,
on the day I married her daughter:
"Have I gained a son?"
and tell her how deeply, gratefully
one can love a second chance.

What is love?

When you are old,
you know how little sense it all makes.
What keeps you going
is a deeply felt oneness,
with Another...
...the answer to the riddle
of elusive human happiness.

When you are old,
choking back all the unshed tears
collected in a lifetime,
your hurt is wiped off
by the smile of one
who forgives you:
imperfect,
not what you pretend
to save your fragile ego
from the rest.

When you are old,
and you have told
all your stories
to anyone who would listen,
your love will gently hold your hand
and ask you to tell, once more,
how you felt
when you met for the first time.

Almost walking

Look at me, Mummy,
I am almost ready to walk,
upright, like you do!
I am working on it so hard,
if I could already talk,
I would ask you:
please tell me
where my road will likely lead
once I take my first unsteady steps on it...

...with my eyes set on the horizon
where dragons and fairies may lurk,
scaring and elating,
but, with you holding my hand,
and smoothing my path,
I am not afraid
of anything!

Memories

It's a maelstrom of swirling images,
a painter's palette gone mad,
dizzying colours, haunting voices,
names, faces, choices...
...memories happy and sad.
I must impose order lest it overwhelm me,
I need to cope with the confusion,
achieve continuity, manage resolution.

I have lived so many lives, all so different,
with tectonic breaks between...
...it's hard to keep track of
what, if anything, connects them,
as I hopped from one existence to another
trying to maintain my balance,
forgetting everything else.

I grew up with humanistic values:
honesty, courage, mutual assistance,
"Treat others as you would have others treat you"
my parents' voice echoes in my mind
with kind, gentle insistence.

The world I knew was confusing,
so many people using each other,
often I couldn't see what they meant...
...but I discovered science - it never lied to me,
explained the beauty and truth of the universe:
mystery easy to understand,
I never had to pretend - found sanctuary.

But I didn't belong in my country,
that corrupt, twisted world;
couldn't trust our leaders who spoke of brotherly love

while enslaving the masses in poverty, ignorance,
crushing any sign of dissent with brutal intolerance.
Finally, I broke to freedom, leaving all behind,
only to discover that humans are humans
in whatever guise.
They spout the slogans, but insist on profit,
people are pragmatic, not idealist.

Now, near the end of this rollercoaster ride,
I am trying to make sense, figure it all out,
what it has all meant, beyond any doubt,
truth I can take with me to the end.

The one constant I can identify,
what I believed in at each different time:
honesty with myself, courage to face facts,
and the love I always felt
for my soul mates,
for my friends.

Sadness

Gulls soar in the sky

Gulls soar in the sky.
I spread my arms to the wind...
...gravity's my fate.

The path

Death is a distant horizon
when you embark on your quest,
when you want to test your strength,
conquer some peaks...
...the blue ocean, the lava-spewing crater
speak to you with promise of adventure,
you want to venture to the depth of secret caves,
swim with the sharks,
ride an elephant to the jungle,
or, maybe, read your Nobel-prized poem at a recitation
or, at least, discover the laws of gravitation.

You see pain, suffering, injustice among men,
you want to show them how to fix the world,
organize their lives, reduce the waste,
stop the destruction --
never realizing: in your innocent hope
you are not even a distraction
to the powers that be --
you are just an insignificant,
slightly annoying bee in their bonnet...
...but you don't see it yet.

Then you get older, 'wiser' you like to say,
not wanting to admit: you are tired
to the bone of more and more of the same.
You suspect the species is not quite sane
and you should quit before you are fired
before you bore them beyond endurance
you should bury your head deep in the sand
before you reach your death
at the ultimate end.

Conflicting loyalties

In grade seven, dripping with compassion,
Fred and I broke into our lab to rescue the rats...
I alone was caught and grilled for an hour,
urged to tell on my friend
or I would be expelled from the school ...
I kept silent - loyalty made me a loser, a fool.

At nineteen I was called up to the army
to attack the Vietnamese
who never did me any harm,
I refused and had to flee,
leave my family, my friends, my life behind,
rather than become a blind puppet of the state
I chose a different fate.

Later in life, as an engineer,
I was offered a lucrative contract,
to work on weapons of mass destruction...
I chose to teach instead, for pitiful wages,
and my family had to go along,
follow me where I thought I belong.

My teaching career didn't last long.
Because support was minimal;
I didn't have the time and the resources
to teach the best way possible,
I wouldn't support mediocre education...
I had to find a new occupation.

Finally, I accepted a job
in a chemical factory,
but the conflict followed me there:
I was ordered to dump digoxin in our river
and, when I refused, I was shown the door,
out on the street once more.

That was the last straw for my wife,
she had enough of my principles,
my loyalty to my convictions,
so she left me to follow my lonely path...

...and I still do, I have no choice,
I must follow the voice in my mind
that tells me what is right...
the only loyalty I cannot fight.

Counterpoint

My species
invented
death camps,
guillotines,
vivisection,
ethnic atrocity,

but discovered
sonnets,
counterpoint,
impressionism,
microphotography...

...no surprise that
it has evolved
a paranoid
schizophrenic
personality.

Drifting

I drift, slowly, across the globe,
on a light wafer of tectonic plate,
a raft floating on wild currents of red-molten rock:
fiery furnace under my feet.

I breathe in the air, a thin bluish haze,
it protects us all: tiny porcupine quills,
bristling on the skin of our planet,
as we point our heads to the stars.

We live here: ephemera,
painted on a dying world
between the lava underneath
and infinity above...

Not knowing how we got here,
where we are going,
how long we have left...
pretending to be important.

The Universe sparkles brightly
in the blackness of space,
galaxies rush outward on their eternal trip,
riding a cosmic wave
of gargantuan explosion...

In this reality we are but a blink of an eye,
filled with yearning, quests, fears,
tiny pleasures, annoying pain,
blissfully unaware, most of the time,
of our tragic, pathetic insignificance.

Fairy Tales
(inspired by Barbara Kingsolver's "Poisonwood Bible")

My parents misled me,
as a small child,
made me believe in fairy tales:
'the good always wins', they insisted,
'evil doesn't have a chance'.
I believed them, and now I am a neurotic adult,
crying in the night: 'how can people be so wicked?,
why 'god' allows it - it isn't right!
This sharp pain is nauseating, I feel paralyzed,
unable to cope, unable to function,
curl up in the fetal position inside me and wish I died.

I spent decades on a lone quest,
studied all the disciplines to explain:
why can't we "just live"
without hurting, destroying lives.
And then, one day, finally I learned the answer
and it was the best to find,
and, in a curious way,
it has brought peace
to my mind.

We all do what we think needs done
to get our desire:
some need beauty and love
others want possessions,
power, excitement -
most just hope to survive.

And then I realized:
no use pretending that
wild and hungry carnivores
don't roam around us...

...nothing hurts as much
as disappointed expectations,
however unjustified!

My Life

I am not going to pretend to know
how you explain the end.
Is it like a deep sleep you never wake up from?
Is it like you were never born?
Is it like anything we ever knew?
I just don't know what is and isn't true.

Sometimes I think I have been here before
and nothing about it is new or surprising,
often I look at myself and see my father
whom I did see as a giant,
while he was only being me.

The end of me is the end of the universe
that started with the big bang
that could have been started by a god
or by pointless coincidence
of nature's forces acting blindly
following causes and effects
it doesn't make any difference.

Still, the fast-approaching end
terrifies the conscious animal in my mind:
my knees get weak, my breath, hollow, short.
I don't want to go, I don't want to leave behind
all that I love: nature, friends, sunsets, butterflies,
and that incredible friend I have loved all my life,
I don't want to leave, never, never, never...
...I want to live forever.

Existence

Existence is such a tenuous thing:
a knife edge splitting off
future from the past:
the not-yet from the not-any-more,
it doesn't last at all,
just tumbles through our minds
from plans to memories
carrying with it
who we think we are:
a collection of hopes and fears -
one never asks:
if there is a grave
for our everlasting soul?

Ode to the programmer

We are a nameless, faceless crowd
writing code for some useless feature,
we are brilliant, creative and proud
being the soul of a soulless creature.

When they think of us
not seeing our gift of communication,
they think of zeroes and ones,
that go into every compilation.

We are the harbingers of an alien culture
that will soon be smarter than we are,
surpassing shaky human structure
with a precision that goes very far

in replacing humans, full of contradiction,
a new step in marching evolution,
confounding today's conceited prediction
with tomorrow's science fiction.

Sentience

Sentience – a gift from the gods:
vision, awareness, desire to exist, to be,
and you want to share this with your kind
and revel in the beauty of the human mind.

You want to love your species
you want to embrace what's best in them:
the arts and the science, the intelligence,
the ability to tell right from wrong,
you want to belong!

But, alas, you have to filter
so much from their minds,
to see the gem under all that interference...
...it doesn't make any difference,

because you are compassionate,
you see how, despite all the ugliness,
they have a glorious inheritance:
the only example in the universe
of their one-of-a-kind sentience.

Vision

Adjusting the zoom
of my imagination
I can observe anything I like:
anytime, anywhere,
there's no limit,
not even the sky.

I can watch galaxies collide,
black holes sucking in light,
colourful nebulas floating in space,
limitless void: sterile beauty,
peaceful, reverent,
like an abandoned Cathedral.

I notice a blue-white planet
orbiting a star
and wonder how small,
how fragile it looks
out this far.

As I get closer
I fall through the clouds
and fly over the landscape below.
I drink in the colours:
oceans, trees, grass,
golden grain of endless prairies;
pink-grey granite mountains
clawing at the sky;
millions of bluish-white sparks
as I cross from azure day
to indigo night.

One more notch
and I'm close enough to
see the cities, people,
roads, cars, canals,
factory chimneys belching at the sky;
battlefields with white crosses;
bronze statues of generals
who planted them;
magnificent mansions
side by side with the slums,
tin-roof houses,
built of discarded packing crates;
dark-skinned children
scavenging on the dumps;
well-bred youngsters
on the golf course
learning the intricacies
of self-absorbed,
pitiless lives.

As I fly on,
the landscape changes again,
I'm skimming the canopy
of an old-growth jungle
with its bustling life:
monkeys leaping through space,
rainbow parrots dazzling my eyes,
a slithering anaconda hugging a branch,
armored alligators floating like logs
on a slow-moving river,
winding its way to where it must -
This picture, too, has death, fear, pain
but still, it is clean, balanced,
does not fill me with a sense of doom,
impending disaster.

One more notch, and
I am watching a colony of termites
like the inside of a Swiss watch
when it was an art
to make things work flawlessly,
with relentless precision
like the passage of time.
Perfect order,
machine-tooled by billions of years of evolution
separating transient from everlasting
until it hit upon the idea
of subjecting the parts to the whole...

...It feels so right,
I can't help wondering
what the world would be like
if 'god' had stopped
on the fifth day:

...then,
His creation would be perfect.

it would be Art.

Wisdom

We live, ascending a mountain,
clambering up a spiral path -
we get back to the same spot again,
a little higher each time,
with a bit more to see.

After a while,
you can't help but see a pattern:
survive, propagate and pass on,
make room for the next cycle,
the next young, blind, groping generation
who will reinvent the same world
in their brash, confident, all-knowing way.

Once you see this,
you're a free man:
not consumed by passion
to understand god's 'Grand Design',
not seeking the holy grail of
'essence', purpose', 'meaning' of life.

And then, with your new-found truth,
you finally open your eyes
to the only thing that matters
and can never be grasped, understood or defined:
the beauty of this wonderful world,
of this magnificent planet...
...waiting to be seen, worshipped
in awe, in humble gratitude and admiration.

Anger

Climate Change

The climate is changing,
and we are changing too:
from ignorance we moved to denial...
...who could think of survival
in the middle of this plenty we see?
Don't ask us to be intelligent,
we are too arrogant to believe in science...
...we have our religion and our-faith-in-progress
for our guidance.

Our children, whom we value most in life,
are in for a nasty surprise
when the shit hits the fan
but that's all right
because we don't give a damn about
what comes after we are gone,
so long as we can have our fun
today.

Dentist

In the dentist's chair
I whimper politely
to let him know he is torturing me.
He ignores it
and keeps digging in deeper,
as if trying to see
how much I can stand.
It would be unfair
to bite his hand,
or scream at him as I'd like to;
having to cause me pain
probably hurts him more
than it hurts me.

Through this fog of horrible ache
I can't help wondering
if this is the fate of the writer:
having to beg people
not to harm him
(please,
don't trash the world
we're all living in)

What if, once, I surprised my dentist
and instead of the pitiful cries,
suddenly I roared like a wounded tiger
and bit his hateful hand really hard?

If I were a brave man
I know what I should do,
to make people listen:
I should climb up on a rooftop
and start shooting at them.

Afterward, I would be on TV,
interviewed by a noted reporter,
who would ask me how I felt
when I pulled the trigger.
I would then tell him: I did it
to wake up the world,
to beauty, truth, danger
and I was careful not to hurt anyone
and I do love my fellow men.

But he would dig deeper until it hurt
just like my friendly dentist
and, instead of a pathetic whimper,
since I had nothing to risk,
I would grab his hand holding the mike
and after a satisfying bite
shove it down his throat
to silence my pitiful voice
that all can hear...
...but to which
no one would listen.

Euthanasia

I killed a child once:
her small, fragile body
convulsing, in helpless agony,
in the middle of the night.

It was the hardest
I ever had to do:
plastic bag over the head,
pillow over tiny body...
tears soaking my face,
resolute till the end,
until the struggle stopped
and, finally, she was dead.

It was 'only' a cat
but I loved her like a child,
loved her enough
to end her pointless suffering.

While most of us would
end the agony
of those we love,
and would want the help
when finally we'll need it --
our rulers say you can't be
merciful to humans -
only to animals,...
they warn of abuse,
criminal negligence.

They fear exceptions,
they are afraid to think, to decide,
they feel safe with zero tolerance:
the hallmark of the craven
and the incompetent.

Death Penalty

Sick bodies, sick minds
dwell in the midst of us.
Sick bodies we cure if we can,
isolate if we must -
killing them would be:
murder.

Sick minds, we hate, fear, destroy,
in cold, methodical ways,
brushing aside pleas for mercy,
cries for compassion,
and only 'god' can forgive us
if we made a mistake:

Our victim is past forgiveness.

Fair Trade

In wars
we trade with the enemy:
left arm for a right eye,
burnt face for a kidney,
orphans for orphans,...
it's not always a fair trade
but the one who was counting
is already dead.

It's all so practical,
supply lines for
our tools:
shells, bullets,
gas for our trucks, tanks,
and our flame throwers too...
paper clips, pencils, official forms
that need to be filled in
with the names of the dead.

Surgeons operate
on conveyor belt
of young people,
so full of blood...
and we don't always have
the right kind
to fill them up,
help them to kill
more boys,
on the wrong side,
heroic dead.

Our pilots drop bombs
on your village,
in exchange for the same...
our wives will weep for us,
answered by the sobbing
of your loved ones,
back where you have been
dragged from, or duped,
to come here,
to be crippled or dead.

When it's all over
with nothing accomplished,
our leaders will make
noble speeches
while wreaths will be hung
over crosses in neat rows
in white forests,
flags draped over caskets,
and the heroic wool
over stupid, stupid, gullible minds,
lamenting the fate
of the glorious dead.

Predation

If I believed in 'god'
I would have to hate his "Intelligent Design":

"Eat and be eaten!",
that's the commandment,
obeyed by 'his' creatures:
the lion rips the throat of the zebra,
a pack of wolves tears a deer apart,
the fox devours the rabbit,
the cat 'plays' with the mouse,
praying mantis munches on butterflies,
Venus flytrap digests insects,
humans, on top of the food chain,
kill, use, torture them all,
including their own kind.

If you are a true believer
how can't you see that
it would have been nothing
to your 'omnipotent' 'father'
to base 'his' design of all of us
on photosynthesis?
Did 'he' like pain, fear, suffering?
Is it divine entertainment?
We did not deserve
to be condemned
to live on a planet
dominated by teeth and claws!

This 'design' is anything but intelligent:
wasteful, cruel, inefficient;
needlessly too complicated:
we don't absorb sunlight

as plants do, turning photons to food,
we receive it indirectly
in a parasitic way,
by devouring each other!

No loving 'god' designed us...
blind, evolving nature is our true mother!

Vegetarians

We are the pariahs of this flesh-eating world:
hated, resented, ridiculed, reviled,
our very existence a threat
of maybe losing a steak or a bacon...
...the non-negotiable staple
of unimaginative minds.

They all know where meat comes from:
the barbaric cruelty of factory farms,
abattoirs, chicken-horror-chambers,
processing plants,
industrial fishing,
special torture for baby animals:
goats, lambs, calves.

Oh, they love their science, technology:
computers and iPhones,
jet planes, the Internet, modern medicine,
but when it comes to their
most fundamental need: food
they insist on cruel, barbaric methods of the past.

The technology is there,
we can synthesize meat
in modern factories,
cheaper, cleaner,
without killing, cruelty, suffering
for living beings:
our animal friends,
we treat them as inanimate garbage
until we devour them
in fake-carnivore style.

Children love animals,
get misty-eyed over kittens,
puppies, baby goats, little lambs,
not told what we do to them
where their burgers come from:
"Eat it dear, it comes from
your friendly neighbourhood Mart"

They say:
it's the natural way,
forgetting that we are unnatural
in every other way:
we fight nature
with science, technology...
...not in nature but in cities
we stay.

We are the flesh-eating disease
of this animal world,
not clean, innocent
as true carnivores are
who don't have a choice...
...we, who evolved with science,
left our brains behind
when it comes to
humane philosophy.

War

The nice man from the bank
helped me get a mortgage
I will pay for the rest of my life.
I thanked him for his kindness
as he read the documents
on how I would lose my home,
if I defaulted on a payment,
how I would find myself quickly
on the pavement.

The lady from the government
then gave me a tax bill to pay,
but she wouldn't say
what my punishment would be
if I couldn't come up with the fee.

The car dealer's gentleman was even nicer
as he gave me the key to my car,
telling me how I would cry
if I couldn't meet my obligations
to pay the monthly installations
I wouldn't get, on foot, very far.

The dentist, before he pulled my tooth,
wanted to know how I would pay him for the maim
he was going to do to my gums
to remove this head-splitting pain.

When I lost my job,
they told me to start a business,
don't wait for others to help me with this
misfortune of mine,

try to become independent,
don't count on my government.

I did and ended up making money
for everyone who suddenly appeared,
taking all that I made:
for rent and for interest,
for penalties, fees, taxes,
for permits and licenses,
for lawyers, for accountants,
for bribes and for promotion,
for legal resolution...
...urging me to work harder,
tighten my belt,
stop complaining about
how it felt.

I thanked them all for helping me along,
with kind words, inspiring phrases,
never once thinking that I was in a war
with a heartless, shameless whore:
the parasites of capitalism,
the leeches of the monied class,
who own our government, make our laws,
who are just happy to eat me alive
never, for a second, shy;
ready to discard me
when sucked dry.

Despair

Farewell song

We exist in a deep cavernous void
studded with galaxies and stars
flitting about like swarms of fireflies
blinking in and out, emitting our cries.

We try to communicate, with smoke signals,
lanterns, acoustic vibrations,
but we are all blind and deaf
to each other's revelations.

We are locked inside our insectoid minds
crawling about our tiny patch of dirt,
never realizing how pointless a quest
it is to be human and not to be hurt.

In our isolated, brief existence,
we are cursed by a hopeless desire
to be loved and understood
that is all we aspire to achieve

as we pass each other
in the middle of the night...
...all we manage in the end
is hurt each other and fight.

It is best to look the other way,
pretending to be completely alone...
...in the midst of a crowded world
lock ourselves inside our home.

We tell ourselves
that loneliness is better than pain
as we hang on to what we call
beautiful, true, humane and sane.

I had a dream last night

I had a dream last night:
I was a tree in pre-hominid times:
a giant red cedar
hugging the earth and the sky,
watching the birds and clouds float by,
stretching my leafy branches in leisurely comfort,
with not a care in the world,
knowing I would never die.

Then I was a bird,
a soaring condor,
being one with the sky
between the earth far below
and infinity above,
as I would fly over granite peaks,
desert dunes,
looking for food, mate,
landing on dewy meadow.

Then I was a whale,
embraced by the sea, the salty waves,
as I dove, and then rose again,
to emerge from the water,
celebrate the sunshine above
and the translucent green below,
wanting to live, in this splendour,
for ever and ever.

I was on the peak in every dream,
no one to hunt me, kill me, no one to fear...
...not knowing that
the end of this beautiful existence
was soon, very soon,
here.

Most people

Most people I know are mostly nice, most of the time.
They work hard, pay their bills,
kind to their neighbours, their pets, their kids,
they do not want to cause any harm.

But, when it comes to thoughts
on politics, religion, social organization,
they haven't got a clue
beyond what's poured on them by the media.
Most don't know how to process information...
...it wasn't a subject in their education.

It's not their fault —
dark forces are lined up against us,
by those who don't want us to know
how our lives on Earth could be simple and beautiful.

Oh, no, they want citizens confused and dutiful,
paying their taxes, rocking no boats,
propaganda rammed down their throats
so they can't possibly form their own thoughts.

Those of us who know what's going on
are helpless in helping the masses --
the victims will fight you tooth and nail,
that's how tough the task is,
every effort that you make will fail.

After a while, you don't even try --
who enjoys to fry on the flames of ignorance?
Write your poetry that no one reads
hoping to plant a few desperate seeds.

The prospector

The prospector is old,
dim eyes searching for elusive glitter,
gnarled fingers still looking for gold,
but all he finds is useless litter.

He thinks he will give it up soon,
abandon this futile obsession,
stop humming this haunting tune,
extinguish a life-long passion.

It's hard to know what new role
he might find in a hopeless life,
not looking for gold in their soul,
accepting the dullness and spite.

Television

I am watching television.
Muted,
as the only way I'm able
to survive the experience.

Skipping channels,
seeking something
good about humanity,
about life.
Something to love,
to admire,
anything to look up to,
be proud of.

I tell myself:
I will add voice
when I see something
I dare
take a chance on.

As I skip on,
I see faces
distorted in hate and anger;
eyes that bulge out;
mouths opened into black holes
of shrill tirades;
fists raised,
swiftly passing blows;
adding pain to fear
of a cowering victim.

Guns aimed;
knives plunged;
bombs exploding
into blinding, searing,
orange and red
pyrotechnics...
...or just plain sadistic
leer of anticipation
of a would-be rapist
over a defenceless
body or mind...

Each blow
lands on my face.
Each wound
mutilates me.
Every angry face
and every malicious smile
burns holes into
my defenses -

How could I survive
sound added to that?

Ugliness

Whenever I am depressed
over the 'human condition';
when the world seems so hopelessly
hell-bent on its own destruction;
drowning in hate, ugliness and stupidity -
I play a mental game I invented
so I'm able to want to live,
so I'm able to forgive and forget.

Imagine the ugliest slum,
squalor, poverty and desolation,
and then mentally remove
item after item,
all objects and artefacts
that belong to men...
...then, when you're done
and have nothing left
but the Globe with all its naked inhabitants,
then you know what Paradise
we were given
when this cosmic experiment started -
then you know what's still underneath
of all you want to forget...

(...yes, I know,
we did not invent
this Darwinian nightmare:
there is violence, pain, fear and suffering
built into the nature of creation;
however, we humans were the first
to create ugliness
where there was nothing
but the splendour of grass, trees, sunsets,
springs, lakes, majestic mountains
and ever-lasting oceans
before...)

The simplest things

The simplest things are, by far, the hardest to see:
we'd rather drown in complications;
when we could just simply, happily, be,
we choose to suffer in self-created abominations.

We invent ideologies, wars, financial meltdowns
when all we need to do is produce,
distribute and consume what we really need
and stop making so many mouths to feed.

Bears, wolves, elk are smarter:
hunt and forage for survival
without trashing their habitat...
...they are not, like us, suicidal.

We waste our enormous brains
on weapons of mass destruction,
and drag the bears, wolves and elk with us
into our self-created mass extinction.

Why?

Why am I trying to say
what so many already said
so much better,
so many times?
Our world is doomed,
and we, who can see it,
are not heard -
we must be mute...
...or the others all deaf.

A truth,
a conviction
needs decades of searching,
thinking, analyzing
to form, crystallize
into knowledge.
You can't share it
with anyone
who has not travelled
the same path...
...and yet, we try.

Maybe we write
for each other,
to help us feel
we're not alone,
there are others, our kind,
almost another species
dispersed on the planet...
...as if we were expelled
from our homeland,
for some horrible crime.

We sing ballads,
spin yarn,
write poems, plays, essays,
philosophize
from soap boxes
or thunder from pulpits,
trying to be heard,
to set their souls on fire...
...all we ever do is:
preach to the choir.

Wild Dogs

I saw a pack of wild dogs on TV, the other day,
they brought down a gazelle,
didn't kill it outright but
started feeding,
tearing out chunks of its flesh,
still alive.

It's the gazelle that shocked me most:
head slightly raised,
just watching them,
with almost an interest.

I didn't see hatred,
outrage or moral indignation
in those sad eyes,
I saw only pain, acceptance,
fast fading light.

Not the gazelle,,
nor the wild dogs
knew about evil.
The dogs had to eat
what they could find,
they were hungry,
had pups to feed.

And then I knew:
for carnivores, life is just survival,
by hunting, killing, devouring,
by sheer force or deception...
...they have no choice...

...we do.

Extinction

Our ancestors made it,
out of the primordial ooze,
launched life, evolution, intelligence,
and here we are today: the apex of creation,
on the verge of self-annihilation.

Our big brains can solve
abstract mathematical equations,
design intricate and complex structures,
are stuck in the animal's fear of starvation
and we think that greed is the only possible solution.

So we replace the simple task of living
with complicated games of domination,
squandering our resources in wars and destruction,
never realizing, even for a second:
we are digging the graves
of our own extinction.

www.ingramcontent.com/pod-product-compliance
Lightning Source LLC
Chambersburg PA
CBHW062004040426
42447CB00010B/1905